mathematics

Minilessons for Extending Multiplication and Division

A Yearlong Resource

CATHERINE TWOMEY FOSNOT

WILLEM UITTENBOGAARD

DEDICATED TO TEACHERS™

361 Hanover Street
Portsmouth, NH 03801–3912
firsthand.heinemann.com

Offices and agents throughout the world

ISBN 13: 978-0-325-01103-5
ISBN 10: 0-325-01103-6

ISBN 13: 978-0-15-360577-2
ISBN 10: 0-15-360577-4

© 2007 Catherine Twomey Fosnot

The development of a portion of the material described within was supported in part
by the National Science Foundation under Grant No. 9911841. Any opinions, findings,
and conclusions or recommendations expressed in these materials are those of the
authors and do not necessarily reflect the views of the National Science Foundation.

Library of Congress Cataloging-in-Publication Data
CIP data is on file with the Library of Congress

Printed in the United States of America on acid-free paper

17   ML   8 9

Acknowledgements

Photography

Herbert Seignoret
Mathematics in the City, City College of New York

Schools featured in photographs

The Muscota New School/PS 314 (an empowerment school in Region 10), New York, NY
Independence School/PS 234 (Region 9), New York, NY
Fort River Elementary School, Amherst, MA

Contents

Contents *Continued*

The Double Number Line and the Ratio Table 57

Extras Just for Fun 69

Overview

Unlike many of the other units in the *Contexts for Learning Mathematics* series, which consist of two-week sequences of investigations and related minilessons, this unit is meant to be used as a resource of 77 minilessons that you can choose from throughout the year. In contrast to investigations, which constitute the heart of the math workshop, the minilesson is more guided and more explicit, designed to be used at the start of math workshop and to last for ten to fifteen minutes.

This guide is structured progressively, moving from the use of graph paper arrays, to the introduction of the open array but with graph paper provided as support, to the eventual use of the open array solely to represent students' strategies for multiplication and division. The latter section of the guide makes use of the number line and the ratio table instead of the array to support proportional reasoning but includes context to help students realize what they are doing. Although you may not use every minilesson in this resource, you will want to work through it with a developmental progression in mind.

The minilessons in this unit are crafted as groups of computation problems designed to encourage students to look to the numbers first, before they decide on a computation strategy. The minilessons will support your students in developing a variety of mental math strategies as well as an understanding of the traditional algorithms. These tightly structured series, or "strings," of problems are likely to generate discussion of certain strategies and big ideas underlying an understanding of multiplication and division. They can also be used with small groups of students as you differentiate instruction.

The Mathematical Landscape: Developing Numeracy

Before you begin working with this unit, try an experiment. Calculate 76 × 89. Don't read on until you have an answer.

If you are like most people who are a product of the American school system, you probably got a pencil and paper, wrote the numbers down in columns, multiplied 6 × 89 (starting with 6 × 9, regrouping the 5 tens and adding it to the product of 6 × 8, for a partial product of 534), then multiplied by the 7 (starting with 7 × 9, regrouping the 6 tens, adding it to the product of 7 × 8, then recording a zero to reflect place value, for a partial product of 6230), and finally added the partial products (starting with the units), for a total of 6764. To check yourself, you probably went back and repeated the same actions and calculations; if you got the same answer twice, you assumed your calculations were correct.

Now take out a piece of graph paper and draw a rectangle that represents a 76 × 89 array. See if you can find the smaller rectangular arrays inside this big one that represent the steps you did as you calculated. If this is difficult for you, the way the algorithm was taught to you has worked against your own conceptual understanding of multiplication.

Students make any number of place value errors in calculating the answer to each of these separate steps, either in regrouping the tens or in lining up the numbers. Why? Just think how nonsensical these steps must seem. Although multiplication is usually introduced in grade three, fourth and fifth graders are often still struggling to understand that 76 × 89 actually means 76 groups of 89—or when envisioned in an array, 76 rows of units (such as square tiles) with 89 units (tiles) in each row. Because students treat the numbers in each step of the problem as digits, they lose sight of the quantities they are actually multiplying.

Liping Ma (1999) compared the way Chinese and American teachers think about and teach the multiplication algorithm and how they work with students who make place value mistakes. Most Chinese teachers approach the teaching of the multiplication algorithm conceptually. They explain the distributive property and break the problem up into the component problems: 76 × 89 = (70 + 6) × (80 + 9) = (6 × 9) + (6 × 80) + (70 × 9) + (70 × 80) = 54 + 480 + 630 + 5,600. Once this conceptual understanding is developed, they compare the steps in the algorithm with the component parts in the equation. (The diagram shows these rectangles, representing partial products, within the larger array of 76 × 89.)

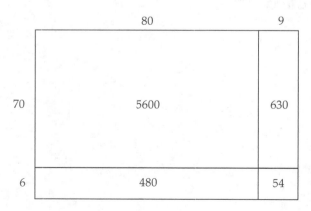

In contrast, 70 percent of American teachers teach the algorithm as a series of procedures and interpret students' errors as a problem with regrouping and lining up. They remind students of the "rules," that they are multiplying by tens and therefore need to move their answer to the next column. To help students follow the "rules" correctly, they often use lined paper and suggest that students use zero as a placeholder (Ma 1999). Sometimes they even resort to teaching the lattice method (an Italian method introduced to Europe by Fibonacci in 1202, and now included in some U.S. curricula) to ensure that fewer place value mistakes will be made.

When students are invited to invent their own ways to decompose the problem—when they have not been taught the algorithm—they usually employ a form of the distributive property naturally! Constance Kamii (1993) found that when she asked students to solve double-digit multiplication problems like 76 × 89, most students began with the largest component. For example, they would break 76 × 89 into 70 × 80 and 6 × 80 and then add the remaining 70 × 9 and 6 × 9. The algorithm, though, requires starting with the units. Kamii, in fact, suggests that teaching algorithms can be harmful to students as they have to give up their own meaning-making just as they are constructing the distributive property in order to adopt the teacher's procedures.

Let's listen in as Sophie, a third grader, tries to make sense of the algorithm in a discussion with Willem Uittenbogaard. They are talking about candies that are sold in rolls of 10.

"How many candies would you have if you had 3 rolls, or 5 rolls, or 7 rolls, or 10 rolls, or 11 rolls?" Willem asks. Sophie easily multiplies by 10 each time. Together they make a table to show the results.

"What if each roll had 11 candies?" Willem then asks. Once again, Sophie responds quickly: "In 3 rolls there would be 33; in 5 rolls, 55; in 7, 77; in 10, 110." But then she pauses. "In 11 . . . I'm not sure. I need paper and pencil." She writes 11 × 11 in column fashion and attempts to perform the algorithm, but she makes a place value error:

$$\begin{array}{r} 11 \\ \times\ 11 \\ \hline 22 \end{array}$$

Looking at her answer of 22, she says, "That can't be." Willem says, "You already know that 10 rolls have 110." Sophie nods, but does not use this information. She writes "11" eleven times in column fashion, and then adds this long column to produce 121. Willem confirms her answer and asks, "What about in 12 rolls?" Once again Sophie asks for paper and pencil and writes:

$$\begin{array}{r} 11 \\ \times 12 \\ \hline 22 \\ 11 \\ \hline 33 \end{array}$$

"Can't be." Again puzzled, Sophie returns to her long column addition and adds another 11 on top. This time, however, she does not add each column but crosses out the 121 and writes down 132, obviously adding 11 to 121 in her head.

Sophie understands that this situation calls for multiplication. She understands that it can be solved by repeated addition. She knows that 10 rolls have 110 candies. She can multiply by 10 easily. She demonstrates that she is aware of the distributive property when she adds one more 11 to 121 (which she even does mentally). She also has a good enough sense of number to know that her answers of 22 and 33 can't be right. Her problem is that the algorithm is getting in the way of her sense-making. She treats the digit 1 in 12 as a unit rather than a 10. She is performing a series of memorized steps (incorrectly), rather than trusting in her own mathematical sense.

It is probably true that if American schools taught the algorithm conceptually rather than procedurally, students would develop a clearer understanding of the process. Teachers could, in fact, build a bridge from students' invented solutions to the algorithm by using the distributive property and rectangular arrays. With Sophie, Willem could write out $12 \times 11 = (2 \times 1) + (2 \times 10) + (10 \times 1) + (10 \times 10)$, build an array, and then look at the pieces of the algorithm, picking them out within the larger 12×11 array. But in today's world, do we want Sophie to have to rely on paper and pencil, or do we want to help her trust in her own mathematical sense and add another 11 to 121? She can do this in her head. Is the algorithm the fastest, most efficient way to

compute? When are algorithms helpful? What does it mean to compute with number sense? How would a mathematician solve 76×89?

Ann Dowker (1992) asked 44 mathematicians to estimate several typical multiplication and division computation problems, one of which was 76×89, and assessed their strategies. Only 4 percent of the responses represented the use of the standard algorithms. The mathematicians looked at the numbers first and then found elegant, efficient strategies that seemed appropriate for the numbers. They made the numbers friendly (often by using landmark numbers), and they played with relationships. Interestingly, they also varied their strategies, sometimes using different strategies to solve the same problems on different days! Most important, they found the process creative and enjoyable.

A common strategy for 76×89 was $(100 \times 76) - (11 \times 76) = 7600 - 760 - 76 = 6764$ (see the rectangular array below). The commutative and distributive properties were employed to make the problem friendlier.

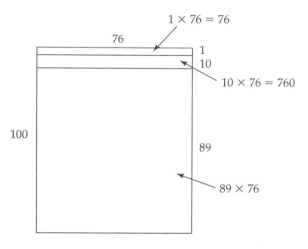

$7600 - 760 - 76 = 89 \times 76 = 6{,}764$

There are many other ways to do this problem. Halving helps. If $100 \times 89 = 8900$, then half of that equals 4450, which is therefore equal to 50×89. To find 25×89, we take half of 4450, which equals 2225. Adding these together, we get $4450 + 2225 = 6675 = 75 \times 89$. Now we just need to add one more 89 to get an answer of 6764. (See the array that follows.)

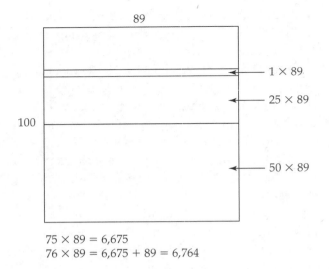

$$75 \times 89 = 6{,}675$$
$$76 \times 89 = 6{,}675 + 89 = 6{,}764$$

Using money sense or fractions is even nicer. Obviously 76 is close to 75, which when thought of in relation to a dollar is ¾, or 75 cents. So ¾ of 89 = 3 × 22.25 = 66.75. Since we divided 75 by 100 to get the original ¾, we now have to multiply 66.75 by 100, which equals 6675, the answer to 75 × 89. Now we need one more 89 to make 76 × 89: 6675 + 89 = 6764.

Or we could make the problem friendly by first working with landmark numbers. We could take 80 × 90 = 7200, then subtract 4 × 90. We now have 76 × 90 = 6840. To get to 76 × 89 we need to subtract one more group of 76. Thus, the final answer is 6764. (See the array below.)

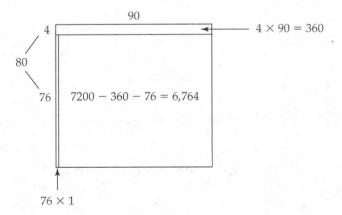

Note how all these alternative, creative ways have far fewer steps than the algorithm and can be done more quickly. Some can be done mentally; others may require paper and pencil to keep track. Playing with numbers like this is based on a deep understanding of number, landmark numbers, and operations, and it characterizes true number sense.

Algorithms can nevertheless be helpful, particularly when multiplying or dividing large, unfriendly numbers of four, five, or six digits. And the beauty of the algorithms is that they are generalizable procedures—they work for any numbers, even large, unfriendly ones. But in today's world, isn't that when we take out the calculator anyway? If we have to reach for paper and pencil to perform the arithmetic, why not reach for the calculator? In most real-world situations, the handheld calculator has replaced paper-and-pencil algorithms.

Does the advance of the calculator mean that students don't need to know how to calculate? Of course not. To be successful in today's world, students need a deep conceptual understanding of mathematics. They will be bombarded with numbers, statistics, advertisements, and data every day—on the radio, on television, and in newspapers. They will need good mental ability and good number sense in order to evaluate advertising claims, estimate quantities, efficiently calculate numbers and judge whether these calculations are reasonable, add up restaurant checks and determine equal shares, interpret data and statistics, and so on. Students need a much deeper sense of number and operation than ever before—one that includes algorithms, but emphasizes mental arithmetic and a repertoire of strategies that allows them to both estimate and make exact calculations mentally.

Depending on the numbers, the algorithm is often slower than other mental arithmetic strategies. It only seems faster to most adults because they have used it for many years. The procedures have become habits that require little thinking. Calculating with number sense as a mathematician means having many strategies available and looking to the numbers first *before* choosing a strategy. How do we, as teachers, develop students' ability to do this? How do we engage them in learning to be young mathematicians at work?

Using Minilessons to Develop Number Sense: An Example

Minilessons are usually done with the whole class together in the meeting area. Young students often sit on a rug; older students can sit on benches placed in a U-shape. Clustering students together like this, near a chalkboard or white board, is helpful because you will want to provide an opportunity for pair talk at times, and you will need space to represent the strategies that will become the focus of discussion. The problems are written one at a time and students are asked to determine an answer. Although the emphasis is on the development of mental arithmetic strategies, this does not mean students have to solve the problems *in* their heads—but it is important for them to do the problem *with* their heads! In other words, encourage students to examine the numbers in the problem and let those numbers guide them in finding clever, efficient ways to reach a solution. The relationships among the problems in each minilesson will support students in doing this. By developing a repertoire of strategies, an understanding of the big ideas underlying why they work, and a variety of ways to model the relations, students are creating powerful toolboxes for flexible and efficient computation. Enter a classroom with us and see how this is done.

Each day at the start of math workshop, Miki Jensen, a fourth-grade teacher in New York City, does a short minilesson on computation strategies. She usually chooses a string of six to eight related problems (like the ones provided in this resource unit) and asks the students to solve them, one at a time, and share their strategies with each other. She allows her students to construct their own strategies for working with numbers in ways that make sense to them. Posted on a strategy wall nearby are signs the students have made throughout the year as they developed a repertoire of strategies for multiplication and division. The signs read, "Make use of money," "Halve and double," "Make use of ten-times," and "When dividing, simplify first." On the chalkboard today as we enter the classroom are Miki's first four problems: 2 × 3, 2 × 30, 4 × 4, and 4 × 40. The students are now engaged in a discussion of the fifth problem, 4 × 42.

Diana, a student in Miki's class, is explaining how she solved the problem: "I know that 4 times 40 is 160, and 4 times 2 is 8. I added and got 168." Miki represents her strategy on an open array:

Diana's math partner Linda, who is sitting next to her, agrees with this answer but used a different strategy: "I just doubled 84. That was 2 times so 4 times is just double that." Miki draws this strategy on an open array as well:

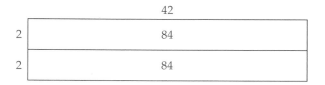

"How many people did this like Linda?" Miki asks, and a few hands go up. "How many of you solved it like Diana?" More hands go up this time. "OK. Turn to the person next to you and convince them that both strategies work." After several minutes of pair talk, Miki asks if there are questions for Diana or Linda. When she sees that there are none, she goes on with her string, writing the next problem, 4 × 39.

"This one isn't so friendly." Miki teases the class with a smile but also offers encouragement: "Take your time. You can use pencil and paper to keep track, but look for a nice efficient way to solve this problem. Show me with a "thumbs-up" signal when you have had enough time." Miki waits until she sees most thumbs up and then she begins discussion. "Alana?"

"I did 4 times 30. That was 120," Alana explains. "Then I did 4 times 9. That was 36. So I added 120 and 36 and got...156." Miki draws an array to represent the partial products.

C.J. nods his head in agreement but says, "I have a shorter way. I used the earlier problem, 4 × 40, and just subtracted 4!" Miki draws the open array shown on page 10 to represent C.J.'s steps and help the other students visualize the parts. "That's pretty neat, isn't it? Who can explain C.J.'s strategy? Diana?"

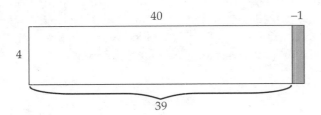

These young mathematicians are composing and decomposing numbers flexibly as they multiply. They are inventing their own strategies. They are looking for relationships among the problems. They are looking at the numbers first before they decide on a strategy. Students don't do this automatically. Miki has promoted the development of this ability in her students by focusing on computation during minilessons with strings of related problems every day. She has developed the big ideas and models through investigations, but once this understanding has been constructed, she builds fluency with computation strategies in minilessons such as this one.

Using Models during Minilessons

As you work with the minilessons from this resource book, you will want to use models to depict students' strategies. Arrays, ratio tables, and number lines are most helpful for multiplication and division. Representing computation strategies with mathematical models provides students with images for discussion and supports the development of the various strategies for computational fluency, but only if the models are understood. Once the model has been introduced as a representation of a realistic situation, you can use it to record the computation strategies that students share with the class. Doing so will enable students, over time, to use the models as powerful tools to think with.

Note: This unit assumes that the models have already been developed with realistic situations and rich investigations. In this series, the *Muffles' Truffles* unit can be used to develop the array model and *The Big Dinner* unit to develop the ratio table. If your students do not fully understand these models, you may find it beneficial to use these units first. Similarly,

since the open number line is the primary model used for addition and subtraction in this series, it is developed in units for earlier grades, *Measuring for the Art Show* and *Ages and Timelines*.

A Few Words of Caution

As you work with the strings and models in this resource book, it is very important to remember two things. First, honor students' strategies. Accept alternative solutions and explore why they work. Use the models to represent students' strategies and facilitate discussion and reflection on the strategies shared. Sample classroom episodes (titled "Inside One Classroom") are interspersed throughout the guide to help you anticipate what learners might say and do and to provide you with images of teachers and students at work. The intent is not to get all learners to use the same strategy at the end of the string. That would simply be discovery learning. The strings are crafted to support development of computational fluency, to encourage students to look to the numbers and to use a variety of strategies helpful for working with those numbers.

Secondly, do not use the string as a recipe that cannot be varied. You will need to be flexible. The strings are designed to encourage discussion and reflection on various strategies important for numeracy. Although the strings have been carefully crafted to support the development of these strategies, they are not foolproof: if the numbers in the string are not sufficient to produce the results intended, you will need to insert additional problems, depending on your students' responses, to support them further in developing the intended ideas. For this reason, most of the strings are accompanied by a Behind the Numbers section describing the string's purpose and how the numbers were chosen. Being aware of the purpose of each string will guide you in determining what types of additional problems to add. These sections should also be helpful in developing your ability to craft your own strings. Strings are fun both to craft and to solve.

References and Resources

Dolk, Maarten, and Catherine Twomey Fosnot. 2005a. *Fostering Children's Mathematical Development, Grades 3–5: The Landscape of Learning.* CD-ROM with accompanying facilitator's guide by Sherrin B. Hersch, Catherine Twomey Fosnot, and Antonia Cameron. Portsmouth, NH: Heinemann.

———. 2005b. *Multiplication and Division Minilessons, Grades 3–5.* CD-ROM with accompanying facilitator's guide by Antonia Cameron, Carol Mosesson Teig, Sherrin B. Hersch, and Catherine Twomey Fosnot. Portsmouth, NH: Heinemann.

Dowker, Ann. 1992. Computational Estimation Strategies of Professional Mathematicians. *Journal for Research in Mathematics Education* 23(1): 45–55.

Kamii, Constance (with Sally Jones Livingston). 1993. *Young Children Continue to Reinvent Arithmetic: Third Grade.* New York, NY: Teachers College Press.

Ma, Liping. 1999. *Knowing and Teaching Elementary Mathematics.* Mahwah, NJ. Lawrence Erlbaum Associates, Inc.

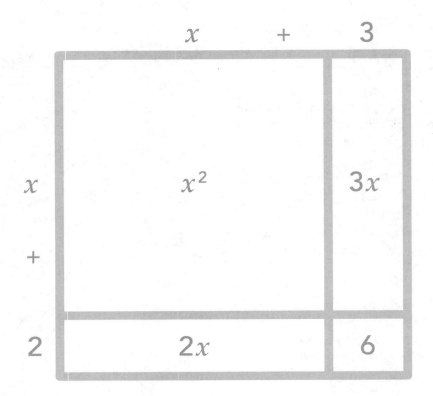

The Array

Rectangular arrays provide a geometric model of the partial products used in the multiplication of two numbers. They can be very helpful in representing the relationship of multiplication to division, in developing an understanding of dimension and area, and in preparing the way for later algebraic work with quadratic equations. At first it is recommended that you use graph paper arrays to ensure that students understand the model, but later you can move to a simple rectangular drawing representing the partial products students offer—an open array.

Doubling, Doubling and Halving

This mental math minilesson uses a string of related problems designed to encourage students to use multiplication facts they know to find the answers to other, more challenging ones. The string also supports use of the strategy of doubling and halving. Do one problem at a time, giving enough think time before you start discussion. Use graph paper arrays and have scissors handy to cut them to match students' strategies. For example, if a student says, "I cut a 6 by 8 in half to make a 12 by 4," cut a 6×8 array into two 6×4 arrays and then place one above the other to make a new array, 12×4.

$$3 \times 4$$
$$3 \times 8$$
$$6 \times 8$$
$$12 \times 4$$
$$24 \times 2$$
$$48 \times 1$$
$$3 \times 16$$

Behind the Numbers: How the String was Crafted

The first three problems are basic facts that are presented one at a time and related in a way to support the use of doubling (each one is double the previous one). The next three problems in the string are all equivalent, because one factor doubles in value while the other halves. Even if students do not use doubling and halving to produce the answers, the fact that the answers are the same may prompt a discussion on equivalence. The doubling and halving is not as easy to see in the last problem, because students must look back over the string to find the corresponding problem. And now, since the answer to the last problem is the same as in the four previous problems, new relationships can be examined. For additional support, see the related strings that follow—A2 and A3.

A Portion of the Minilesson

Inside One Classroom

Miki (the teacher): *(Writes on the chalkboard 6 × 8.)* Here is the next one…another multiplication fact. What is 6 times 8? Chas?

Chas: That's 48.

Author's Notes

Learning the basic multiplication facts is critical when moving on to more challenging multiplication problems.

continued on next page

continued from previous page

Miki: *(Writes 48 next to the problem and puts a 6 × 8 array next to the problem.)* Great, and here's a 6 by 8 array I cut out. Can somebody show us how this is a 6 by 8 array? Megan?

Megan: There's 6 squares going down and 8 going across. *(Points to the rows and columns of the array.)*

Miki: Everybody agrees that we have 6 rows and 8 columns? *(Nods from the class.)* OK, here's another problem. *(Writes 12 × 4 directly underneath the first problem.)* Take a minute to think about how you would solve this problem. When you are ready to share, put thumbs up so you don't disturb other people who are still working on it. *(Waits several seconds before calling on students to share.)* Debbie?

Debbie: Well, I just knew it. I knew 12 × 4 was 48. But I also noticed that it's the same answer as 6 × 8.

Miki: That's interesting, Debbie. Did anybody else notice that? I wonder why that happened.

Claire: I think you double and halve 6 × 8 so it's the same answer.

Miki: Can you say more about that, Claire?

Claire: Um, well, 12 is double 6 and 4 is half of 8 so the answer is still 48.

Miki: *(Draws the following representation:)*

Claire, can you show us how the doubling and halving works using the 6 by 8 array?

Claire: You cut the 6 by 8 array in half. So you count 4 squares across and cut down the line there. *(Uses scissors to cut the 6 × 8 array in half vertically.)* And then you take one of the pieces and connect it to the bottom of the other piece so that you have 12 squares going down. *(Attaches one 6 × 4 piece to the bottom of the other 6 × 4 piece to make a 12 × 4.)* That's a 12 by 4 array now, and you still have 48.

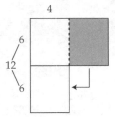

Miki: This is interesting. Let's think about the next problem, and how the array can be doubled and halved using Claire's method. Here it is: 24 × 2. *(Writes 24 × 2 directly under 12 × 4.)*

The use of the array provides students with a representation of their strategies. Eventually the array will become a tool to think with.

One of the reasons that each problem in a string is written directly below the previous one is to encourage students to notice the relationships.

Miki asks Claire to expand on her thinking in order to encourage conversation on this important strategy.

The paper array is cut and moved to represent Claire's strategy.

Miki invites reflection on the strategy.

Graph Paper Arrays · A2

Doubling, Doubling and Halving

See A1 for details (page 13).

2×8

4×8

8×8

16×4

32×2

64×1

32×4

Graph Paper Arrays · A3

Doubling, Doubling and Halving

See A1 for details (page 13).

3×8

6×8

12×8

24×4

48×2

96×1

6×16

3×14

Graph Paper Arrays · A4

Relating Multiplication and Division, Equivalence, Simplifying

This mental math minilesson uses a string of related problems designed to encourage students to use multiplication facts they know to compute answers to division facts that are not yet automatic, by challenging them to examine the relationship between multiplication and division. Do one problem at a time, giving enough think time before you start discussion. Use graph paper arrays, and have scissors handy to cut them to match students' strategies.

$$6 \times 8$$
$$48 \div 6$$
$$48 \div 8$$
$$24 \div 4$$
$$24 \div 3$$
$$12 \div 2$$
$$8 \div 1$$
$$6 \div 1$$

Behind the Numbers: How the String was Crafted

The first three problems are a triplet to lay the foundation for examining the relationship between multiplication and division. The fourth problem is equivalent to the third. As you work through the string, students will have opportunities to examine simplifying to make a friendly equivalent expression, and the relationship of division to multiplication. See A5 for additional support.

Graph Paper Arrays · A5

Relating Multiplication and Division, Equivalence, Simplifying

See A4 for details (page 15).

$$4 \times 12$$
$$3 \times 12$$
$$48 \div 12$$
$$24 \div 6$$
$$12 \div 3$$
$$48 \div 16$$
$$24 \div 8$$
$$12 \div 4$$

Graph Paper Arrays · A6

Commutative Property, Doubling

This mental math minilesson uses a string of related problems designed to encourage students to use multiplication facts they know to figure out other, more difficult problems. The string also supports the use of the commutative property for multiplication. Do one problem at a time, giving enough think time before you start discussion. Use graph paper arrays, and have scissors handy to cut them to match students' strategies.

$$3 \times 8$$
$$16 \times 3$$
$$6 \times 16$$
$$16 \times 12$$
$$6 \times 32$$
$$64 \times 3$$
$$6 \times 64$$

Behind the Numbers: How the String was Crafted

The first three problems are a triplet used to lay the foundation for the focus of the string. It begins with a fact students are likely to know and then introduces relationships among the problems to promote exploration of doubling and the use of the commutative property. A discussion of the commutative property will arise because the factors are reversed at times, making the doubling and halving less apparent. As the string progresses, students will have opportunities to examine doubling further.

Graph Paper Arrays · A7

Relating Multiplication and Division, Doubling

This mental math minilesson uses a string of related problems designed to encourage students to use multiplication facts they know to figure out other, more difficult problems. It also challenges students to examine the relationship between multiplication and division. Do one problem at a time, giving enough think time before you start discussion. Use graph paper arrays, and have scissors handy to cut them to match students' strategies. Division is represented in this string with both the bar and the ÷ to familiarize students with both signs. The bar representation for division will be helpful when students are introduced to fractions.

$$2 \times 12$$
$$4 \times 12$$
$$8 \times 12$$
$$96 / 12$$
$$96 / 8$$
$$96 \div 4$$
$$96 \div 2$$

Behind the Numbers: How the String was Crafted

The numbers in this string have been chosen to allow students to examine the relationships in the answers that exist when the divisor is halved, or when a factor doubles.

Bridging to the Open Array · A8

Associative and Distributive Properties, Multiplication by Ten

This mental math string encourages students to use multiplication facts they know automatically to figure out more difficult problems. This particular string emphasizes the associative property of multiplication and the use of ten-times. Toward the end of the string, students are challenged to make partial products employing the distributive property. Again, do one problem at a time, giving enough think time before you start the discussion. Use graph paper arrays in the beginning, but begin to introduce the open array after the first two or three problems, if students seem able to envision the partial products. Invite students to discuss the relationships among the problems in the string.

$$2 \times 3$$
$$2 \times 30$$
$$4 \times 4$$
$$4 \times 40$$
$$4 \times 41$$
$$4 \times 39$$

Behind the Numbers: How the String was Crafted

The first and third problems in the string are basic facts that are related to the second and fourth problems, respectively. Each pairing supports the development of the associative property. For example, 2×30 can be thought of as $2 \times (3 \times 10)$ or $(2 \times 3) \times 10$. The last two problems in the string support students' move toward understanding the distributive property of multiplication: 4×41 contains one more group of 4 than 4×40. For the last problem, some students might split 39 and do $(4 \times 30) + (4 \times 9)$ and add the partial products together, $120 + 36 = 156$. Other students might notice a connection to the previous two problems. For example, $4 \times 39 = 4 \times (40 - 1) = (4 \times 40) - (4 \times 1)$. If students set up the standard multiplication algorithm (vertically) to solve 4×39, encourage them to think about what is happening mathematically as they use this strategy. For example, when students say, "Then I multiplied 4 with the 3 [from the 30]," ask them to find where the 3 should be placed on the graph paper array. See if they realize that the 3 refers to 3 tens, or 30 and thus the array on the graph paper should be a 4×30. Invite students to make connections between the standard algorithm and other strategies. The standard multiplication algorithm is based on the distributive property, like the previous strategies described above. See A9 for additional support.

A Portion of the Minilesson

Inside One Classroom

Miki (the teacher): Here is the array for 2×3, which Lori just said was 6. *(Displays a precut graph paper array of 2×3 next to the problem.)* I'm going to write another problem on the board. Before you raise your hand, I want you to take a look at it and think about what the array for this new problem might look like. *(Writes 2×30 directly underneath the first problem in the string. Pauses to give students think time.)* Megan?

Megan: It's 60. And I think the array is going to be long and short. *(Gestures with her hands.)*

Miki: *(Displays a precut array of 2×30 next to the problem.)* Megan, how did you get 60? Can you talk about that?

Megan: Well, I knew that $30 + 30$ equals 60. But another way I did is I know that 2×3 is 6, and if you add a zero to the 3, then you just add a zero to the 6.

Miki: Hmmm, but usually when I add zero to a number, my answer is the same. For example, if I add a zero to the 3 here like you said, $3 + 0$ is 3. Are we really adding a zero? What's happening here? *(One or two hands go up. Most students give blank stares.)* OK, turn to a neighbor and talk about this question. What is really happening when we put a zero at the end of the number? Talk to the person next to you about this.

(Students turn to each other to discuss this question. Miki listens in on the different conversations that are taking place. The following is an excerpt from one of these conversations.)

Chas: I think there's 10 of the 2 by 3s. I think that's what it means.

Author's Notes

Notice that Miki does not ask for the answer to 2×30 right away. Instead, she asks students to think about how it would look.

The "adding-zero method" is a trick that students often use when multiplying with ten or multiples of ten. Miki invites students to dig deeper into the workings of this method in order to understand what is happening mathematically. By asking what is really happening when they "add" a zero, Miki has created confusion among the students. This disequilibrium is a necessary step in the development of the mathematics.

Miki provides students with the opportunity to slow down, to reflect on and make sense of something that was previously a rote procedure.

continued on next page

continued from previous page

Miki: Thomas and Joe, what do you think about what Chas just said? Do you agree? Disagree?

Thomas: I agree with Chas.

Miki: Joe, do you think you can restate what Chas said in your own words? Thomas, do you think it would help if Joe also used the arrays to explain what Chas said?

Thomas: Yeah, I'm a little confused.

Joe: *(Turns to Chas.)* Well, I think you said that there's 10 of the 2 by 3s, right? Like if you take the 2 by 3 array, and you count 10 times, it would fit inside the 2 by 30 array.

Miki: Can you show us what you mean by count 10 times? Go ahead and use the arrays on the board.

Joe: See, like you do this. *(Lays the 2 × 3 array on top of the 2 × 30, matching up the rows.)* So that's 1, 2, 3, 4, 5...10. *(Slides the 2 × 3 array across the 2 × 30 array and counts the number of times the 2 × 3 array fits.)*

(Returning to the whole-group conversation.)

Miki: I listened in on an interesting conversation that Thomas, Joe, and Chas were having. Chas, can you represent the group and share what you discussed?

Chas: We noticed that there are ten 2 by 3s in 2 by 30. So if you make ten 2 by 3 arrays, it would add up to 60.

Miki: *(Writes on the board:)*

$$(2 \times 3) \times 10 = 2 \times (3 \times 10) = 60$$

Let's try it. I'm going to draw a line every time we have a 2 by 3 array on the 2 by 30 array. Could you count aloud together?

Class: One, 2, 3, 4...10. *(Miki draws a line for every 2 × 3 array inside the 2 × 30 graph paper array.)*

Miki: That's interesting. So there are ten 2 by 3 small arrays. But it seems amazing when I add 6 + 6 + 6 + 6...10 of them...and I land on a number with a zero on the end...always. Why does this happen?

Chloe: I think it's because you also have 6 tens. You can turn it around: 10 × 6 = 6 × 10. So the number goes to the tens place.

Miki: Oh, that's interesting, isn't it. *(Miki rotates the array 90 degrees to match what Chloe said).* Let's see if that idea helps with the next pair of problems. And this time I'm not going to use the graph paper arrays. Let's just try to envision them and I'll just draw rectangles to match your strategies. *(Writes 4 × 4).*

In addition to the math lesson, Miki is also thinking about how she can support her students in becoming accountable participants during whole- and small-group conversations. She encourages students to ask questions when confused and to clarify their thinking, not for her, but for each other. She wants students to feel responsible to each other, not just to her, the teacher.

Miki does not do the explaining. Students are encouraged to explain their strategies to the community.

A specific case of the use of the associative property is being examined here.

Students often need to physically check the relationship. Miki allows them to do so by using the array and tracking their counting.

The commutative property helps explain why the digits move over a place: 10 x 6 = 6 x 10.

Since the students appear to be able to envision the array of 2 x 30 and the 2 x 3 arrays within, Miki moves towards using the open array.

Associative and Distributive Properties, Multiplication by Ten

See A8 for details (page 18).

4 × 8

4 × 80

5 × 7

5 × 70

5 × 71

5 × 69

Bridging to the Open Array · A10

Associative Property

The problems in this string encourage students to double and halve the factors involved, but then extend this strategy to tripling and thirding and the more generalized use of the associative property. Again, do one problem at a time, giving enough think time before you start the discussion. Use precut graph paper arrays to support student strategies in the beginning if needed. It is assumed at this point that students will be quite comfortable with using the array to depict multiplication and you can start modeling their strategies on the open array. Invite students to discuss the relationships among the problems within the string.

6 × 8

12 × 4

3 × 16

5 × 9

15 × 3

45 × 1

24 × 3

Behind the Numbers: How the String was Crafted

The first three problems in the string are equivalent. The first two will probably remind students of the doubling and halving strategies they have used in previous strings, but the third problem may provide an opportunity for discussion. The factors in the first problem can be doubled and halved to produce the third, but once solved it may also be observed that the second problem could be looked at as a quadrupled and quartered version of the third. The next three problems invite students to consider other strategies for finding solutions such as tripling and thirding. The big idea underlying the reason that these strategies work is the associative property: $(5 \times 3) \times 3 = 5 \times (3 \times 3)$. The last problem requires students to come up with their own friendly problems. Thirding and tripling the factors turns the problem into a fact they know: 8×9. For additional support, see the related strings that follow—A11 and A12.

Bridging to the Open Array · A11

Associative Property

See A10 for details (page 21).

8×6

4×12

2×24

6×8

12×8

6×32

2×96

27×3

Bridging to the Open Array · A12

Associative Property

See A10 for details (page 21.)

8×9

4×18

2×36

4×12

8×12

16×12

4×48

1×192

Associative Property

This string of related problems is crafted to support development of fluency in using the associative property. It encourages students to think about 16×20 as $16 \times 2 \times 10$ or as $16 \times (2 \times 10) = (16 \times 2) \times 10$. Do not expect all students to be able to use the associative property at the start. Record whatever strategies they use on the open array. In this string and the strings that follow, only the open array is used. See Inside One Classroom, page 24 for an illustration. As students begin to notice the patterns that appear in the answers, use the array to explore with them why this is happening. The last problem in the string adds an opportunity for discussing the distributive property, as well.

$$16 \times 2$$
$$16 \times 10$$
$$16 \times 20$$
$$16 \times 4$$
$$16 \times 40$$
$$12 \times 30$$
$$12 \times 32$$

Behind the Numbers: How the String was Crafted

The first three problems are a cluster. Students may simply double the product of the second problem to solve the third problem, but in doing so they may also come to realize the third problem's relationship with the first problem. The next two problems are related similarly. The fourth may also be solved by doubling the product of the first. The fifth provides another opportunity to discuss how helpful the associative property can be. The next problem has no helpers in the string so students have to make their own. The last problem challenges with the addition of an opportunity to make use of the distributive property. If the last two problems are difficult for students, include additional clusters similar to the previous problems. Several additional strings focused on the associative property follow—A14 through A20.

Inside One Classroom

Author's Notes

Chris (the teacher): Jodi, you said that the answer to 16 × 40 was 64 with a zero on the end. Sixty-four was the answer to 16 × 4. This pattern happened before, too, with the first and third problems. Why does this pattern happen? Everybody, turn to the person next to you and talk about this. *(After a few moments of pair talk.)* Carlos, what did you and your partner discuss?

Carlos: We know it happens but we don't know why.

Chris: How many people feel like Carlos? You're pretty sure it works, but you don't know why. *(Many hands go up.)* OK, let's try to figure this out. It is a puzzle, isn't it? I'll draw the 16 by 4 array.

Pair talk involves all the students in considering what is happening and why it is happening. Chris moves around and listens in on some of the conversations, and after a few minutes resumes whole-class discussion.

Chris offers the array as a tool to think with.

How do I turn this into a 16 by 40?

Carlos: Oh, I think I get it. You need 10 of them!

Chris: Let me write what you just said. *(Writes:)*

$$16 \times 40 = 16 \times 4 \times 10$$

Michelle: Yes, he's right! You could also do 16 × 10 × 4.

Chris: *(Writes:)*

$$16 \times (4 \times 10) = (16 \times 4) \times 10 = (16 \times 10) \times 4$$

Let's think about this and let me get a picture up of the array that Carlos is talking about.

Chris does not acknowledge that Carlos is correct. Instead he draws a representation for the community to consider. Ideas hold up as "truth" when they make sense.

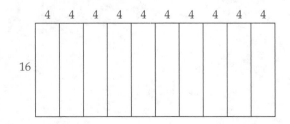

Associative Property

See A13 for details (page 23).

3 × 7

6 × 7

36 × 7

18 × 14

28 × 18

56 × 36

Behind the Numbers: How the String was Crafted

This string begins with two basic facts that remind students of the doubling strategy. The second problem (6 × 7) can be thought of as $2 \times (3 \times 7) = (2 \times 3) \times 7$, although students will probably just know the answer. The third problem requires students to think of the relationship between 6 and 36. Many students may use partial products here (30 × 7 + 6 × 7); others may use the relationship between 6 and 36, i.e., 6 × (6 × 7). The fourth problem is equivalent to the third, as one factor has doubled and the other has halved. The last two problems build on a variety of the problems in the string. Encourage students to examine the relationships and to decompose factors to simplify. For example, 56 × 36 is just 8 × 7 × 36, and 7 × 36 has already been solved. And, 28 × 18 is just twice the value of 18 × 14.

Associative Property

See A13 for details (page 23).

4 × 7

8 × 7

24 × 7

8 × 21

42 × 8

42 × 40

7 × 240

Associative Property

See A13 for details (page 23).

4 × 9

8 × 9

24 × 9

8 × 27

27 × 16

27 × 80

9 × 240

The Open Array · A17

Associative Property

See A13 for details (page 23).

14 × 2

14 × 10

14 × 20

70 × 4

70 × 40

22 × 40

23 × 40

Associative Property

See A13 for details (page 23).

4 × 9

12 × 3

36 × 1

9 × 12

27 × 4

3 × 36

18 × 6

15 × 12

Behind the Numbers: How the String was Crafted

The first three problems in the string are equivalent; students may notice the tripling and thirding pattern readily. The next four problems become more challenging; each one pushes students toward efficient mental computation. To solve the fourth problem, 9×12, students may use the partial products of 90 and 18. Thirding and tripling may be used to solve the problem that follows. Some students may begin to notice that $3 \times 36 = 3 \times (4 \times 9) = (3 \times 4) \times 9$ and $18 \times 6 = (3 \times 6) \times 6 = 3 \times (6 \times 6)$. In order to solve the final problem in the string, students must come up with their own friendly equivalents. For example, students might try thirding and tripling right away, arriving at 5×36, based on their earlier work. This may still be difficult for some to tackle without paper and pencil. Five, however, is always a friendly number to work with since it is half of ten. Using doubling and halving, the problem can be made quite friendly: $10 \times 18 = 180$. Students can also begin by tripling and thirding in this way, 45×4, and then doubling and halving to get $90 \times 2 = 180$.

The Open Array · A19

Associative Property

See A13 for details (page 23).

9 × 5

3 × 15

1 × 45

2 × 45

4 × 45

2 × 90

20 × 90

The Open Array · A20

Associative Property

See A13 for details (page 23).

9 × 8

3 × 24

1 × 72

2 × 72

4 × 72

4 × 144

8 × 72

The Open Array · A21

Commutative Property, Place Value, Multiplication by the Base

This string is designed to help students examine what happens when they multiply by powers of ten: 100, 1000, etc. Again, introduce one problem at a time, giving enough think time before you start the discussion. Use the open array to model student strategies and help students realize the mathematical meaning of what they are doing. Encourage students to share what they notice about the relationship of the number of zeroes in the answers to the number in the factors. As you progress through the string, examine how the commutative property helps explain what students often refer to as the "zero trick." The zero pattern seems amazing in the repeated addition of 10 sevens, but when students realize that because of the commutative property the problem is also 7 tens, they can easily understand why the 7 moves to the tens place.

$$1 \times 7$$
$$10 \times 7$$
$$7 \times 10$$
$$100 \times 7$$
$$1,000,000 \times 7$$
$$7 \times 1,000,000$$
$$1 \times 35$$
$$10 \times 35$$
$$1000 \times 35$$

Behind the Numbers: How the String was Crafted

The problems in the string all involve multiplication by a power of ten. This illustrates special properties because the number system is a base ten system. In some successive problems the same factors appear, but in reverse order. When students notice that the answers to these problems are identical, they have an opportunity to consider how the commutative property of multiplication is involved. The commutative property is interspersed to provide opportunity to examine not only the place value patterns that occur, but why they occur.

The Open Array · A22

Commutative and Associative Properties, Place Value, Multiplication by the Base

This string is similar to A16 but both factors are now multiples of ten. Although one can still consider the commutative property as an explanation for the pattern of zeroes, the associative property is also helpful. For example 10×10 can be thought of as: $1 \times 10 \times 10 = 1 \times 100$.

$$10 \times 10$$
$$10 \times 100$$
$$100 \times 100$$
$$1000 \times 1000$$
$$1000 \times 10,000$$
$$1000 \times 123$$
$$100 \times 1230$$

Behind the Numbers: How the String was Crafted

The first three problems are related in that in each subsequent case an original factor has been increased by a factor of ten and thus the product increases by a factor of ten. The fourth and fifth problems increase the product of the third problem by a factor of 100, and then 1000, respectively. The last pair is provided to support students to consider how the associative property is involved: $1000 \times 123 = (100 \times 10) \times 123 = 100 \times (10 \times 123)$.

The Open Array · A23

Relating Multiplication and Division, Place Value

This string is designed to help students examine what happens when they divide by a power of ten: 100, 1000, etc. Again, introduce one problem at a time, giving enough think time before you start the discussion. Use the open array to model student strategies and help students realize the meaning of what they are doing. Encourage students to share what they notice about the relationship of the number of zeroes in the quotient, to the number in the divisor and dividend.

$$350 \div 10$$
$$3500 \div 100$$
$$35{,}000 \div 10$$
$$1{,}000{,}000 \div 100$$
$$1{,}000{,}000 \div 1000$$
$$1{,}000{,}000 \div 10{,}000$$
$$1{,}000{,}000 \div 100{,}000$$

Behind the Numbers: How the String was Crafted

The problems in the string all involve division by a power of ten. Using powers of ten in both the dividend and the divisor supports an examination of the place value involved. The array and the relationship between the dividend and divisor can help students realize the magnitude of these large numbers.

The Open Array · A24

Distributive Property, Landmarks More or Less, Using Partial Products

This mental math minilesson uses a string of related problems to encourage students to examine partial products and to compose and decompose numbers using them. The use of ten-times is emphasized by using just one group more or one group less. Do one problem at a time, eliciting several student strategies and recording them on the open array. Invite students to examine the different strategies and discuss the connections they notice among the problems.

$$10 \times 13$$
$$11 \times 13$$
$$9 \times 13$$
$$20 \times 13$$
$$21 \times 13$$
$$19 \times 13$$
$$101 \times 13$$

Behind the Numbers: How the String was Crafted

The problems are in clusters of threes to support the use of partial products. For example, the first problem is the foundation for the second and third, the answers to which are each one group of 13 away from the answer to the first problem. The last problem in the string requires students to examine the numbers and make the partial products themselves.

The Open Array · A25

Distributive Property, Landmarks More or Less, Using Partial Products

This mental math minilesson uses a string of related problems similar to A24 to encourage students to examine partial products and to compose and decompose numbers using them. The difference from A24 is the use of landmarks 100, 200, 1000. As always, do one problem at a time, seeking several student strategies and recording them on the open array. Invite students to examine the different strategies and discuss the connections they notice among the problems.

$$100 \times 15$$
$$101 \times 15$$
$$99 \times 15$$
$$110 \times 15$$
$$200 \times 15$$
$$201 \times 15$$
$$1001 \times 15$$
$$999 \times 15$$

Behind the Numbers: How the String was Crafted

The first three problems are a cluster; the first problem is the foundation for the second and third, which are each one group away (more or less) from the first. The fourth problem challenges with the addition of ten-times (using the distributive property). The next two problems are related; the first of these two provides support for solving the second. The last two problems in the string require students to analyze the numbers and make the partial products themselves.

The Open Array · A26

Multiplication with Landmark Numbers

This mental math minilesson uses a string of related problems with landmark numbers, specifically 25, 100, and 50. Do one problem at a time, seeking several student strategies and recording them on the open array. Invite students to examine the different strategies and discuss the connections they notice among the problems.

$$4 \times 25$$
$$16 \times 25$$
$$400 \times 25$$
$$1600 \times 25$$
$$30 \times 100$$
$$30 \times 50$$
$$32 \times 50$$
$$33 \times 50$$
$$84 \times 50$$

Behind the Numbers: How the String was Crafted

The first four problems are designed to encourage students to consider 25 as a landmark. Starting with 4×25 lays the foundation for considering 25 as a quarter of 100. Then 50 can be considered as either twice the quarter of 100, or as half of 100. The remaining problems in the string provide students opportunities to make use of these relationships.

The Open Array · A27

Division with Landmark Numbers, Doubling, Equivalence, Using Partial Quotients

This mental math minilesson for division uses a string of related problems with landmark numbers, specifically 25, 100, and 50. Do one problem at a time, seeking several student strategies and recording them on the open array. Invite students to examine the different strategies and discuss the connections they notice among the problems.

$$100 \div 25$$
$$200 \div 25$$
$$200 \div 50$$
$$400 \div 25$$
$$400 \div 50$$
$$1600 \div 25$$

Behind the Numbers: How the String was Crafted

The first problem is the helper as it provides the landmark. All the remaining problems in the string can be made easier with the use of this landmark expression. It can be used as a partial quotient and added twice to solve the second problem, or as an equivalent expression to the third. Analyzing the relationships in the answers will enable students to consider the equivalence in the problems. The second answer is double the value of the first. The third is equivalent to the first. The fourth is double the second, etc. The last problem in the string provides a useful challenge. Invite students to consider that the 1600 can be decomposed into 1000 and 600. The partial quotients ($1000 \div 25$ and $600 \div 25$) can be made friendlier by making use of the problems already solved in the string—for example $1000 \div 25$ is 10 times the quotient of the first problem, and the quotients of the second and fourth problems can be added to solve $600 \div 25$. In turn, the partial quotients of $1000 \div 25$ and $600 \div 25$ can be added to determine $1600 \div 25$.

The Open Array · A28

Distributive Property, Using Partial Products

This mental math minilesson uses a string of related problems to encourage students to examine partial products and to compose and decompose numbers with them. The use of ten-times is emphasized. Do one problem at a time, seeking several student strategies and recording them on the open array. Invite students to examine the different strategies and discuss the connections they notice among the problems.

7×6

10×6

17×6

20×7

2×7

22×7

24×7

43×7

Behind the Numbers: How the String was Crafted

The problems are in clusters to support the use of partial products. For example, the first two problems can be used to make the third; the seventh problem can be solved with the fourth and twice the fifth, or with the fifth and sixth, etc. The last problem in the string requires students to make the partial products themselves, yet the fourth or sixth problem may provide some support. For additional support, see the related strings that follow—A29 and A30.

The Open Array · A29

Distributive Property, Using Partial Products

See A28 for details (page 33).

9×8

10×8

19×8

20×8

3×8

23×8

26×8

49×8

The Open Array · A30

Distributive Property, Using Partial Products

See A28 for details (page 33).

7 × 9

10 × 9

17 × 9

20 × 9

5 × 9

25 × 9

30 × 9

37 × 9

The Open Array · A31

Associative and Distributive Properties, Relating Multiplication and Division

This string of related problems is crafted to support development of fluency in using the associative and distributive properties. It encourages students to think about 12 × 60 as 10 × 60 + 2 × 60, and 20 × 60 as 2 × 10 × 60. It also provides an examination of the fact that the distributive property does not hold for division, where 60 ÷ 10 + 60 ÷ 2 does not equal 60 ÷ 12.

10 × 60

2 × 60

12 × 60

20 × 60

60 ÷ 10

60 ÷ 2

60 ÷ 12

600 ÷ 12

Behind the Numbers: How the String was Crafted

The first four problems form a cluster to lay the foundation for examining the distributive and associative properties. Division problems follow. Students often assume that since the distributive property holds for multiplication, it holds for division as well. They are usually surprised to realize that this is not so. To divide 60 by 12, they could divide by 3 and then divide that quotient by 4, or they could distribute the dividend and divide each portion of it by 12, e.g., $(48 + 12) \div 12 = 48 \div 12 + 12 \div 12$ because of the distributive of multiplication over addition. But they cannot distribute $60 \div 12$ into $60 \div 10 + 60 \div 2$ and produce the quotient of $60 \div 12$. If the last two problems are difficult for students, insert more clusters like the previous problems. The purpose of this string is to support students in examining how the dividend can be distributed as the distributive property of multiplication is employed, but the divisor can not be. See A32 for additional support.

The Open Array · A32

Associative and Distributive Property, Relating Multiplication and Division

See A31 for details (page 35).

$$600 \div 5$$
$$600 \div 20$$
$$600 \div 25$$
$$600 \div 4$$
$$600 \div 20$$
$$600 \div 24$$
$$150 \div 6$$

The Open Array · A33

Factoring the Divisor, Relating Multiplication and Division

This string of related problems is crafted to examine factoring the divisor. One can factor the divisor and use the factors in helpful ways. For example, consider the problem, $60 \div 12$. Because 2 and 6 are factors of 12, the quotient of $60 \div 12$ can be found by dividing the quotient of $60 \div 6$ by 2.

$$12 \times 60$$
$$3 \times 60$$
$$4 \times 180$$
$$60 \div 3$$
$$20 \div 4$$
$$60 \div 12$$
$$600 \div 12$$
$$960 \div 12$$

Behind the Numbers: How the String was Crafted

The first three problems provide an example of factoring. The next three problems allow students to explore its use as a strategy for division. The last two problems in the string require students to consider their own choice of helpers: 960 could be divided first by 2 and then that quotient by 6; or by 3 and then that quotient by 4, etc.

The Open Array · A34

Revisiting the Associative and Distributive Properties

This string of related problems is crafted to revisit the use of the associative and distributive properties. It encourages students to think about 12×20 as $12 \times 2 \times 10$, or as $12 \times (2 \times 10) = (12 \times 2) \times 10$. Record whatever strategies students use on the open array.

$$12 \times 2$$
$$12 \times 10$$
$$12 \times 20$$
$$4 \times 60$$
$$40 \times 60$$
$$22 \times 40$$
$$23 \times 41$$

Behind the Numbers: How the String was Crafted

The first three problems are a cluster. Students may just double the product of the second problem to solve the third problem, but in doing so they may also come to realize the third problem's relationship with the first problem. The next two problems are related similarly. The fourth may be solved by doubling the product of the second, or realizing it is equivalent to the third. The fifth provides a chance to discuss how helpful the associative property can be. The next problem has no helpers in the string so students have to make their own. The last problem challenges with the addition of an opportunity to make use of the distributive property. If the last two problems are difficult for students, include additional clusters similar to the previous problems. See A35 for additional support.

The Open Array · A35

Revisiting the Associative and Distributive Properties

See A34 for details (page 37).

$$5 \times 9$$

$$5 \times 90$$

$$6 \times 8$$

$$6 \times 80$$

$$6 \times 81$$

$$7 \times 80$$

$$7 \times 79$$

The Open Array · A36

Distributive Property of Multiplication over Subtraction

Difficult multiplication problems such as 32×29 can be thought of as $32 \times (30 - 1) = (32 \times 30) - (32 \times 1)$. The problems in this string are crafted to encourage the development of this strategy. This does not mean, however, that all students will use this strategy—only that it is likely to come up in discussion as you progress through the string. Do one problem at a time and encourage students to share the strategies they use. Represent these using open arrays. Facilitate discussion on the relationships among the problems. An array drawn to show the distributive property of multiplication over subtraction is shown below. This example shows 19×14:

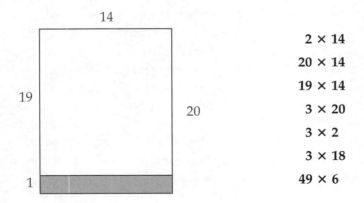

$$2 \times 14$$

$$20 \times 14$$

$$19 \times 14$$

$$3 \times 20$$

$$3 \times 2$$

$$3 \times 18$$

$$49 \times 6$$

Behind the Numbers: How the String was Crafted

The first six problems in the string are clustered into two sets of triplets. Each set has two helper problems that can be used to solve the more difficult third problem. The last problem requires students to construct their own helper problem—for example, 50 × 6. For additional support, see the related strings that follow—A37 and A38.

The Open Array · A37

Distributive Property of Multiplication over Subtraction

See A36 for details (page 38).

3 × 15

30 × 15

29 × 15

3 × 30

3 × 3

3 × 27

39 × 5

The Open Array · A38

Distributive Property of Multiplication over Subtraction

See A36 for details (page 38).

4 × 12

40 × 12

39 × 12

4 × 40

4 × 4

4 × 36

58 × 4

Behind the Numbers: How the String was Crafted

The first six problems in the string are clustered into two sets of triplets. Each set has two helper problems that can be used to solve the more difficult third problem. The last problem requires students to construct their own helper problem—for example, 60×4. In contrast to the last problem in A36 and A37, this problem challenges students to deal with the removal of two groups rather than one.

The Open Array · A39

Relating Multiplication and Division

This minilesson uses a string of related multiplication and division problems as a way to encourage students to use multiplication to solve division problems. The open array is also used to model division strategies. Arrays are powerful models for developing an understanding of how the operations of multiplication and division are related. Whereas arrays with multiplication are initially drawn with both dimensions labeled, in division a proper modeling of the situation has only one dimension labeled and the dividend is labeled as the area of the array. The array also allows you to represent partial quotients (or partial products) and represent them as parts of the larger array as students use the distributive property for multiplication.

$$12 \times 10$$
$$120 \div 12$$
$$120 \div 10$$
$$36 \div 12$$
$$12 \times 13$$
$$156 \div 12$$
$$169 \div 13$$

Behind the Numbers: How the String was Crafted

The first three problems are designed to encourage students to consider the relationship of multiplication and division right at the start. The fourth problem will probably be easy and it can be helpful in connection with the next two problems. The last problem can be made easy by using the problems before it. For additional support, see the related strings that follow—A40 and A41.

The Open Array · A40

Relating Multiplication and Division

See A39 for details (page 40).

17×10

$170 \div 10$

$170 \div 17$

$34 \div 17$

12×17

$204 \div 17$

$187 \div 17$

The Open Array · A41

Relating Multiplication and Division

See A39 for details (page 40).

21×10

$210 \div 10$

$210 \div 21$

11×21

$231 \div 21$

$231 \div 11$

$121 \div 11$

The Open Array · A42

Distributive Property of Multiplication over Addition with Division, Partial Quotients, Standard Long-Division Algorithm

This string of related problems is designed to encourage students to look at partial quotients and to consider how they can be combined to determine quotients of related numbers. This string can be used to build a connection to the standard long-division algorithm. Do one problem at a time. Accept a variety of strategies but encourage students to look for relationships among the problems. Record student strategies using open arrays, as described in Inside One Classroom, page 42.

$$21 \div 3$$

$$30 \div 3$$

$$51 \div 3$$

$$81 \div 3$$

$$140 \div 14$$

$$154 \div 14$$

$$280 \div 14$$

$$294 \div 14$$

Behind the Numbers: How the String was Crafted

The first two problems are helpful for solving the third. The fourth can be solved using the second and third, or with twice the second problem plus the first. The dividend of the sixth contains just one more group of 14 than does that of the fifth. The last two problems are related similarly. You may find it helpful to discuss the connection between this string and the standard long-division algorithm because the partial quotients in this string are the numbers used in the procedure. For additional support, see the related strings that follow—A43 and A44.

Inside One Classroom

A Portion of the Minilesson

Author's Notes

Chris (the teacher): So here is the third one, $51 \div 3$. Show me with a "thumbs-up" when you are ready. *(After a few minutes.)* Billie?

Billie: I used the first two problems. That made it easy.

Chris: Oh, that was helpful! I'm going to draw the arrays of what you said.

	10	7
3	30	21

But I also want to represent your idea another way, because sometimes mathematicians write the pieces down as they go along and subtract to keep track. You might see people write it this way sometimes, too.

```
        17
    3 ) 51
        30      10
        21       7
        21
```

Chris represents the partial quotients on the open array but he also represents the long-division algorithm. Here the representation is matched to Billie's strategy. It is not being taught as a procedure to use for all problems (even though it is generalizable) because sometimes it is not the most efficient strategy. On the other hand, it is important for students to have the option of using it, when they need or want to.

The Open Array · A43

Distributive Property of Multiplication over Addition with Division, Partial Quotients, Standard Long-Division Algorithm

See A42 for details (page 41).

$$24 \div 4$$
$$40 \div 4$$
$$64 \div 4$$
$$104 \div 4$$
$$130 \div 13$$
$$143 \div 13$$
$$260 \div 13$$
$$273 \div 13$$

The Open Array · A44

Distributive Property of Multiplication over Addition with Division, Partial Quotients, Standard Long-Division Algorithm

See A42 for details (page 41).

$$28 \div 7$$
$$70 \div 7$$
$$98 \div 7$$
$$168 \div 7$$
$$170 \div 17$$
$$187 \div 17$$
$$340 \div 17$$
$$357 \div 17$$

The Open Array · A45

Distributive Property of Multiplication over Addition or Subtraction with Division, Partial Quotients

This string of related problems is designed to encourage students to look at partial quotients and to consider how they can be combined to determine quotients of related numbers. In contrast to the standard algorithm, the distributive property for multiplication over subtraction is also employed. Do one problem at a time. Accept a variety of strategies but encourage students to look for relationships among the problems. Represent student strategies using open arrays.

$$140 \div 14$$
$$28 \div 14$$
$$168 \div 14$$
$$154 \div 14$$
$$280 \div 14$$
$$294 \div 14$$
$$266 \div 14$$

Behind the Numbers: How the String was Crafted

The string begins with a division problem requiring the use of 10×14 to emphasize the use of ten-times for division. The first two problems are helpful partial quotients for the third. The fourth problem and the sixth one are easier to solve if students think of removing a group of 14. The last problem provides a substantial challenge with 2 groups of 14 removed. For additional support, see the related strings that follow—A46 through A50.

The Open Array · A46

Distributive Property of Multiplication over Addition or Subtraction with Division, Partial Quotients

See A45 for details (page 43).

$$160 \div 16$$
$$32 \div 16$$
$$192 \div 16$$
$$176 \div 16$$
$$320 \div 16$$
$$352 \div 16$$
$$304 \div 16$$

The Open Array · A47

Distributive Property of Multiplication over Addition or Subtraction with Division, Partial Quotients

See A45 for details (page 43).

$$180 \div 18$$
$$36 \div 18$$
$$216 \div 18$$
$$198 \div 18$$
$$360 \div 18$$
$$396 \div 18$$
$$342 \div 18$$

The Open · Array A48

Distributive Property of Multiplication over Addition or Subtraction with Division, Partial Quotients

See A45 for details (page 43).

$$270 \div 27$$
$$297 \div 27$$
$$243 \div 27$$
$$135 \div 27$$
$$540 \div 27$$
$$408 \div 34$$

The Open Array · A49

Distributive Property of Multiplication over Addition or Subtraction with Division, Partial Quotients

See A45 for details (page 43).

$$350 \div 35$$
$$385 \div 35$$
$$315 \div 35$$
$$175 \div 35$$
$$700 \div 35$$
$$840 \div 70$$

The Open Array · A50

Distributive Property of Multiplication over Addition or Subtraction with Division, Partial Quotients

See A45 for details (page 43).

$$410 \div 41$$
$$451 \div 41$$
$$369 \div 41$$
$$205 \div 41$$
$$820 \div 41$$
$$861 \div 41$$

The Open Array · A51

Revisiting the Distributive Property for Multiplication Again, Using Partial Products

This next set of strings revisits the distributive property for multiplication. It is helpful for students to revisit multiplication periodically while working on division to remind them of the relationship between the operations. This string is designed to encourage students to examine partial products and to compose and decompose numbers flexibly. Do one problem at a time and record students' strategies on the open array.

$$10 \times 127$$

$$127 \times 2$$

$$12 \times 127$$

$$10 \times 44$$

$$9 \times 44$$

$$9 \times 43$$

$$8 \times 43$$

Behind the Numbers: How the String was Crafted

The first two problems in the string will probably be easy for your students. The third problem is more difficult, but the products of the first two can be used to derive the third. The fifth problem can be done by using the fourth one and removing a group of 44. It is assumed that students will be quite comfortable at this point with using distributivity, but the last three problems may provide a challenge as students need to consider carefully how much to subtract—44, 43, 9, 8, or 10. For additional support, see the related strings that follow—A52 and A53.

Inside One Classroom

A Portion of the Minilesson

Carol (the teacher): Here's our first warm-up problem. Thumbs-up when you have an answer. Michael?

Michael: It's 1270. I just know. I used the pattern of multiplying by tens.

Carol: *(Draws the following representation of Michael's strategy:)*

	127
10	1270

Does everyone agree with Michael? *(No disagreement is apparent.)*
So it's 127 tens? OK. Let's go to the next one: 127×2. Emmy?

Emmy: 254. I doubled the 100 and then doubled the 27.

Carol: How many people did it like Emmy? *(Several hands go up.)*
What other ways are there? Sean?

Author's Notes

Carol begins with two problems that are quite easy for her students. She uses them only to provide the partial products that may be used for the third problem.

continued on next page

continued from previous page

Sean: I thought of it as 125 twice, like a dollar and a quarter. So 250, plus 4.

Carol: What do you think? Does Sean's way work? I'll make the array.

The array is drawn to provide an image of the strategy for discussion.

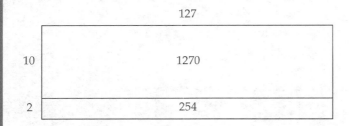

Suzanne: Yes. He just broke up the pieces differently than Emmy.

Carol: OK, let's try this one: 12 × 127. You can keep track on paper if you need to. Remember, mental math doesn't have to be in your head, just with your head!

The students are not expected to draw the arrays, but over time the model will become a tool to think with.

Kathie: I just put the last two problems together.

Carol: Nice. I'll make a picture of what you said.

```
          127
┌──────────────────────┐
│                      │
10│        1270         │
│                      │
├──────────────────────┤
2 │         254          │
└──────────────────────┘
```

Carol uses the open array to represent Kathie's use of the partial products.

Carol: Here's our next one: 10 × 44. And since I know you all know this one, I'll just make a picture. See if you can use the picture to do 9 × 44.

```
        44
┌──────────────────┐
10│      440         │
└──────────────────┘
```

Amanda: I think you take a group of 10 away.

Carol: What do you all think? Is Amanda right—you take away a group of 10? Turn to the person next to you and talk about this.

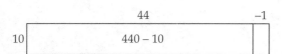

The array model provides a focus of discussion. Deciding what to remove is difficult and here the students are encouraged to reflect with pair talk. Discussing each other's strategy develops a sense of risk-taking and community.

(After pair talk, whole-group conversation resumes.)

Amanda: No, I was wrong. You have to take away 44, not 10. it should be 9 rows of 44, not 10 rows of 43.

Carol does not avoid the error. Instead she explores it and conversation continues until the community determines an agreed-upon answer. In this case that means removing a group of 44, not 10.

The Open Array · A52

Revisiting the Distributive Property for Multiplication Again, Using Partial Products

See A51 for details (page 46).

10 × 125

4 × 125

14 × 125

10 × 58

9 × 58

9 × 57

8 × 57

The Open Array · A53

Revisiting the Distributive Property for Multiplication Again, Using Partial Products

See A51 for details (page 46).

10 × 126

126 × 2

12 × 126

10 × 49

9 × 49

9 × 48

8 × 48

The Open Array · A54

Simplifying before Dividing, Proportional Reasoning

This string of related problems encourages students to explore how it is sometimes easier to simplify before dividing. Do one problem at a time, recording students' strategies on the open array. If you notice students beginning to make use of equivalent problems as you progress through the string, invite a discussion on how helpful that strategy can be. If the class comes to a consensus that this is a helpful strategy, you might want to make a sign about this. The sign can then be posted on a "strategy wall." The main big idea underlying this strategy is proportional reasoning. Two types of division signs are used here to remind students that the signs are interchangeable. The bar representation will be helpful when students work with fractions, and fraction equivalence.

$$100 \div 4$$
$$200 / 4$$
$$200 / 8$$
$$400 \div 16$$
$$300 / 12$$
$$600 \div 24$$

Behind the Numbers: How the String was Crafted

The string has been crafted to support simplifying (or reducing) as a strategy for whole-number division. The quotient in the second problem is twice the quotient in the first because the dividend is twice the value of that in the first problem, while the divisor stays the same. In the third problem, the divisor doubles in value and the dividend stays the same. The quotient is thus half of the quotient in the second problem, but now equivalent to the quotient in the first problem. Relationships like this occur throughout the string. Encourage students to discuss the relationships they notice and to explore what happens to the quotients. For additional support, see the related strings that follow—A55 through A59.

A Portion of the Minilesson

Inside One Classroom

Lisa (the teacher)**:** So let's start today with 100 ÷ 4. Show me with thumbs-up when you are ready. Sally?

Sally: It's 25. I just thought of it as quarters, money.

Lisa: I bet a lot of you did. Yes? OK. Let's just go on to the next one. How about 200 ÷ 4?

Joanne: It's twice as much.

Lisa: Let me draw an array. Here's the first problem:

	25
4	100

So now we have twice as much inside, but still four rows. Let's see what that array would look like.

continued on next page

Author's Notes

Lisa knows that most of her students have a good sense that there are four quarters in a dollar so she does not spend much time here. Instead, she moves on to the harder problems in the string.

The open array is drawn as a model that can be varied and used as a tool to explore the relationships among the problems as the string continues.

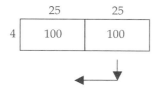

What about this one: 200 ÷ 8? Turn to the person next to you and talk about this one. Also talk about what you think the array will look like.

Josh: I know the answer is half of the last answer. I'm not sure about the array.

Maria: I think it just moves down.

Lisa: What moves down?

Maria: The last array, the 100. It moves down and over.

Lisa: *(Draws array with an arrow.)*

Pair talk is used to provide time for thinking and for reflection. Students are also encouraged to picture how the array will change.

As the class works on the rest of the string, the arrays will be used to investigate the relationships between the problems. Equivalence in the problems will also be established— for example, 200 ÷ 8 = 100 ÷ 4.

The Open Array · A55

Simplifying before Dividing, Proportional Reasoning

See A54 for details (page 49).

$$100 \div 5$$
$$200 \div 5$$
$$200 \div 10$$
$$400 \div 20$$
$$300 \div 15$$
$$1200 \div 60$$

The Open Array · A56

Simplifying before Dividing, Proportional Reasoning

See A54 for details (page 49).

$$300 \div 6$$
$$600 \div 6$$
$$600 \div 12$$
$$1200 \div 24$$
$$900 \div 18$$
$$1800 \div 36$$

The Open Array · A57

Simplifying before Dividing, Proportional Reasoning

See A54 for details (page 49).

$$60 \div 2$$
$$120 \div 4$$
$$240 \div 8$$
$$480 \div 16$$
$$960 \div 32$$
$$240 \div 16$$
$$2400 \div 160$$
$$3600 \div 120$$

Behind the Numbers: How the String was Crafted

The first five problems are all equivalent. This structure will cause students to wonder why the answer is the same each time. The sixth problem invites them to consider a case when both dividend and divisor do not increase proportionally. The last problem in the string has no helper problems so students must make their own. As students progress through the problems in the string, encourage them to think about how the arrays are related—for example, $120 \div 4$ is equivalent to $240 \div 8$ in that the quotient—the number of columns in the array—stays the same. In other words, the number of elements in the array and the number of rows change, but the number of columns stays the same. Students may be confused that the arrays are not congruent, and it is important to focus them on how the numbers of columns are equivalent.

The Open Array · A58

Simplifying before Dividing, Proportional Reasoning

See A54 for details (page 49).

90 ÷ 3

180 ÷ 6

360 ÷ 12

720 ÷ 24

1440 ÷ 48

720 ÷ 12

7200 ÷ 120

5600 ÷ 80

The Open Array · A59

Simplifying before Dividing, Proportional Reasoning

See A54 for details (page 49).

80 ÷ 4

160 ÷ 8

320 ÷ 16

640 ÷ 32

1280 ÷ 64

640 ÷ 16

6400 ÷ 160

4800 ÷ 120

Using the Difference of Squares, Distributive Property, Using Partial Products

This mental math minilesson is designed to examine how one square number differs from the next succeeding square number. Do one problem at a time, recording students' strategies on the open array.

$$10 \times 10$$
$$11 \times 10$$
$$11 \times 11$$
$$20 \times 20$$
$$20 \times 21$$
$$21 \times 21$$
$$60 \times 60$$
$$61 \times 61$$
$$80 \times 80$$
$$81 \times 81$$
$$101 \times 101$$

Behind the Numbers: How the String was Crafted

The first six problems consist of two sets of triplets designed to support students in producing the partial products needed to examine the difference in consecutive squares. The change in the factors that generate the second problem results in an increase of 10 from the product of the first problem, and the third is an increase of 11 from the second. The increase in the product of the first problem to the third is thus 10 plus 11. A similar pattern is repeated in the next triplet. The next four problems are in two sets of pairs. One intermediary problem has been removed in each case, and students need to consider what it would be. The last problem is a challenge. No related problems are provided, but students may find that thinking of 100×100 might be helpful as a partial product.

Using the Difference of Squares, Distributive Property, Using Partial Products

This mental math minilesson is designed to examine how one square number differs in value from others. It is likely to become an inquiry. Have students work in pairs and use calculators if needed. Ask students to examine the patterns in the answers and draw arrays to show why the patterns are occurring. This string does not have supports as do other strings in this guide, however the patterns in the answers prove interesting!

$$5 \times 5$$
$$15 \times 15$$
$$25 \times 25$$
$$35 \times 35$$
$$45 \times 45$$
$$55 \times 55$$
$$65 \times 65$$
$$95 \times 95$$
$$105 \times 105$$

Behind the Numbers: How the String was Crafted

The last two digits in every answer are 2 and 5. There is also an interesting pattern in the tens column. In 35×35, for example, the digit in the tens place of each factor is 3. Add 1 to it. Now it is 4. The product is 1225. Note that $4 \times 3 = 12$. Examine $25 \times 25 = 625$. Note that $3 \times 2 = 6$. The partial products that explain this pattern are $30 \times 40 + 25$ and $30 \times 20 + 25$, respectively. Use arrays to explore why these partial products are made. Does one need to have 5×5? What if the numbers were 34×36? You might find it fun yourself to get out graph paper and explore these questions.

The Open Array · A62

Using the Difference of Squares, Distributive Property, Using Partial Products

This mental math minilesson is designed to examine the ways in which squares can be helpful in making some unfriendly problems friendly. Have students work in pairs and use calculators if needed. Ask students to examine the patterns in the answers and draw arrays to show why the patterns are occurring. Students are probably not familiar with order of operations, so the parentheses have been added as a support. Explain that what is in parentheses should be done first.

7×5

$(6 \times 6) - 1$

9×7

$(8 \times 8) - 1$

8×12

$(10 \times 10) - (2 \times 2)$

7×13

$(10 \times 10) - (3 \times 3)$

19×21

18×22

17×23

Behind the Numbers: How the String was Crafted

The string is structured in pairs of equivalent problems to develop the following strategy: find the midpoint between the two factors and square it. Now find the difference between the two factors, divide it by 2, and square this amount. The difference between the two square numbers is the product of the original problem. The mathematics here can be represented as $(x + y)(x - y) = x^2 - y^2$. Do not ask fourth and fifth graders to represent these relations with algebraic symbols. However, as students explore with arrays, the focus of the inquiry should be on explaining, and showing with arrays, the way that the partial products are distributed. For example, consider 17×23 on an array. We could represent it as $(20 - 3) \times (20 + 3)$, as shown below.

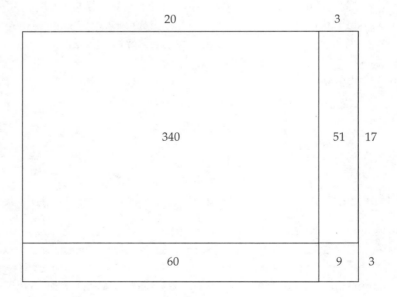

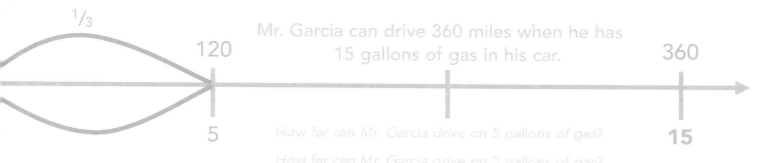

Mr. Garcia can drive 360 miles when he has
15 gallons of gas in his car.

How far can Mr. Garcia drive on 5 gallons of gas?
How far can Mr. Garcia drive on 3 gallons of gas?

Gallons	Miles
15	360
5	120
3	72

The Double Number Line and the Ratio Table

The double number line and the ratio table are powerful models for representing multiplicative thinking and proportional reasoning. With several of the strings in this section, you can use either model or both. The number line is perhaps a more concrete model since the measurement can be illustrated in steps or jumps. Some of the strings use only this model. Each string indicates which model or models are appropriate to use with it.

Materials Needed for this Section

Large chart pad and easel (or chalkboard or whiteboard)

Markers

Double Number Line or Ratio Table · B1

Keeping the Ratio Constant in Division, Proportional Reasoning

This string of related problems encourages students to examine division problems as expressions represented on a number line, or a ratio table. A double number line is an effective way to represent the relationships between the problems, or you can use a ratio table, such as a t-chart. Write one problem at a time and ask students to give a thumbs-up when they know the answer. When several thumbs are up, start discussion. Ask students to explain their reasoning, and represent the strategy on the open number line. Then ask for other strategies for the same question and have students compare them. Then move to the next problem. Invite students to discuss the connections among the problems and record these relationships. As you progress through the string, if you notice students beginning to discuss equivalence, invite a discussion on how such equivalence could help solve division problems. For additional support, see the related strings that follow—B2 and B3.

$$36 \div 6$$
$$72 \div 6$$
$$72 \div 12$$
$$144 \div 24$$
$$42 \div 6$$
$$126 \div 18$$
$$425 \div 25$$

Behind the Numbers: How the String was Crafted

The first four problems are related. The first problem is likely to be an automatic fact for students, but by starting the string with it you can quickly represent 6 jumps of 6 units, landing at 36 on the number line. Students will probably realize that the answer to the second problem is double the value of the answer to the first problem. You can then write $2 \times (36 \div 6) = 72 \div 6$ and represent the relationship on an open number line, as shown below:

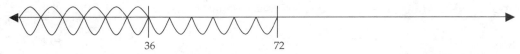

If students do not immediately double the jumps, the partial quotients they use can also be represented on the double number line. For example, if a student uses the standard long-division algorithm, making use of $60 \div 6$ and $12 \div 6$, you can represent it as follows:

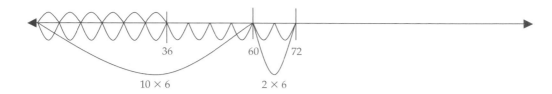

The third problem is equivalent in value to the first. Even if students do not initially realize or make use of the relationships, the relationships of the problems in the string and the representations on the double number line will support them in exploring these equivalencies. The figure below represents $72 \div 12 = 36 \div 6$. It is still 6 jumps, but in a 2 for 1 ratio.

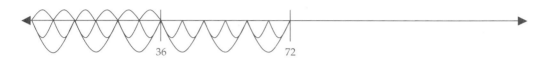

A Portion of the Minilesson

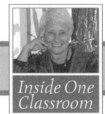

Inside One Classroom

Author's Notes

Carlos (the teacher)**:** OK. So the first one was easy. How about this one? Who has $72 \div 6$? Show me with thumbs-up when you're ready. *(After most thumbs are up.)* Sharon?

Sharon: It's 12. The first one was 6 and this one is just double, because 72 is double 36.

Carlos: Let me represent what you said on the number line. *(Represents 6 jumps of 6 twice under the line: 6 groups of 6 are already on top of the line.)* So can I write this? *(Writes:)*

By using the number line and by writing the equation, Carlos provides his students with a visual representation of the equation.

$$(2 \times 36) \div 6 = 72 \div 6$$

Turn to the person next to you and discuss this.

Pair talk is important here to ensure that everyone is involved in considering the equivalence.

Monique: Two of those fit into one.

Juan: Yeah.

Carlos: It's helpful to look at relationships in problems, isn't it? How about this one next: $72 \div 12$.

Mathematicians look for and use equivalent relations. Carlos encourages his students to do the same.

Monique: It's half of the last one.

Thomas: Yeah. It's the same as the first one, too, because 6 is twice 12—no, I mean if you double 6 you get 12 and if you double 36 you get 72. So it's the same. It's 6 again.

continued on next page

continued from previous page

Carlos: So, Thomas, if I draw 6 sixes like this on the number line and then think of each jump as a 12, like this, then 6 twelves are double 36?

Thomas: Yeah, that's what I mean. Each 6 becomes a 12 down below. It's still 6 jumps. They're just twice as big.

The representations drawn reflect student strategies.

Double Number Line or Ratio Table · B2

Keeping the Ratio Constant in Division, Proportional Reasoning

See B1 for details (page 58).

42 ÷ 7

84 ÷ 7

84 ÷ 14

168 ÷ 28

36 ÷ 9

72 ÷ 18

300 ÷ 15

Double Number Line or Ratio Table · B3

Keeping the Ratio Constant in Division, Proportional Reasoning

See B1 for details (page 58).

48 ÷ 6

96 ÷ 6

96 ÷ 12

192 ÷ 24

81 ÷ 9

162 ÷ 18

600 ÷ 40

Proportional Reasoning

This string (and the subsequent ones) makes use of a context of gallons of gas per unit of distance. As such it is different from the other strings in this guide in which pure number was the focus. The context is used to examine proportional relationships with a double number line. Because the context suggests distance, a number line is more helpful to use here than a ratio table. Do one question at a time, collecting multiple strategies and representing them on a double number line with the number of miles on top and number of gallons on the bottom. For example, if students say that 5 gallons is a third of the way, so that is ⅓ of 360, you would draw the following:

Mr. Garcia can drive 360 miles when he has 15 gallons of gas in his car.

How far can Mr. Garcia drive on 5 gallons of gas?

How far can Mr. Garcia drive on 3 gallons of gas?

How far on 8 gallons?

How far on 4 gallons?

How far on 1 gallon?

**How many gallons of gas would Mr. Garcia
need in order to drive 600 miles?**

Behind the Numbers: How the String was Crafted

The first problem makes use of the landmark number of five. Also, 360 is a number for which it is fairly easy to find ⅓. These three portions (the 120 for each of the thirds) can then be marked on the double number line. The second problem brings up the relationship between multiplication and division: ⅓ of 15 = 5; ⅕ of 15 = 3. The third problem can be solved by adding the results of the first two problems. The next problem is half of that result. As the string continues, students will probably begin to use a variety of relationships.

Double Number Line or Ratio Table · B5

Remainders, Proportional Reasoning

This mental math minilesson uses a string of related context problems with remainders. Students must decide what to do with the remainder, given the context. Representing the proportional relationships on the number line may support students in making that determination. Do one question at a time, collecting answers and representing them on a double number line or in a ratio table. For example, when answering how many sacks can be filled with 100 marbles if 12 marbles are in a sack, if students say that 60 marbles makes 5 full sacks, 36 marbles makes 3 more, and there are only 4 marbles left, not enough to make another full sack, you might draw the following:

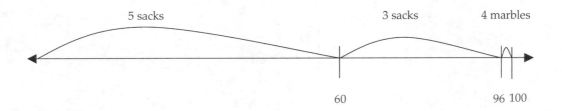

If you are using a ratio table you might represent it as follows:

Number of Marbles	12	60	36	96
Number of Sacks	1	5	3	8

100 marbles, 12 in a sack. How many sacks can you fill?

50 dollars, 8 dollars per ticket. How many tickets can you buy?

50 dollars to share among 8 people. How much does each person get?

160 students going on a field trip, 60 per bus. How many buses should be ordered?

105 cents, 10 cents in a dime. How many dimes in 105 cents?

105 cents, 5 cents in a nickel. How many nickels in 105 cents?

105 cents, 100 cents in a dollar. How many dollars in 105 cents?

Behind the Numbers: How the String was Crafted

Context is used to influence how the remainder should be treated. The first problem requires rounding down; only eight full sacks can be made. The second problem also requires rounding down. The third problem uses the same numbers but now the remainder is also distributed: each person gets $6.25. Juxtaposing the second and third problems was purposeful in order to generate a conversation on why the answers are different. The fourth problem needs to be rounded up; three buses are needed. The last three problems are related and challenge students to consider the relationship of nickels to cents, dollars to cents, etc.

Double Number Line · B6

Remainders, Partial Quotients

This string uses a quotative model of division to examine partial quotients. Explain that the divisor is the length of the jumps. Represent student strategies on a double number line. For example, the following represents $12 \div 4 = 3$.

When exploring $13 \div 4$, you might write $12 \div 4 + \frac{1}{4}$, or $12 \div 4$, remainder 1.

$$12 \div 4$$
$$13 \div 4$$
$$22 \div 7$$
$$28 \div 9$$
$$31 \div 10$$
$$91 \div 30$$
$$76 \div 25$$
$$301 \div 100$$

Behind the Numbers: How the String was Crafted

The first problem introduces equal sharing in juxtaposition to all the other problems in the string, which have a remainder of one.

Double Number Line · B7

Remainders, Relating Multiplication and Division

This string uses a quotative model of division to examine division with remainders. Explain that the divisor is the length of the jumps. Represent student strategies on a double number line. Students are challenged to determine the missing dividend, when supplied with the divisor and the quotient.

$$32 \div 8$$

$$\square \div 8 = 4 \text{ remainder } 2$$

$$\square \div 10 = 4 \text{ remainder } 2$$

$$\square \div 25 = 4 \text{ remainder } 2$$

$$\square \div 30 = 4 \text{ remainder } 2$$

$$\square \div 50 = 4 \text{ remainder } 2$$

$$\square \div 100 = 4 \text{ remainder } 2$$

$$602 \div \square = 4 \text{ remainder } 2$$

Behind the Numbers: How the String was Crafted

The first problem introduces equal sharing in juxtaposition to all the other problems in the string, which have a remainder of two. Here students need to consider the relationship of multiplication and division: the divisor times the quotient, added to the remainder, produces the dividend. The last problem challenges students to reverse the process: to subtract the remainder from the dividend first.

Double Number Line · B8

Relating Multiplication and Division, Doubling and Halving, Associative and Commutative Properties

This string uses a quotative model of division to examine the relationship between multiplication and division. Explain that one factor tells how long the jump is on the number line. The other, missing factor is the number of jumps needed to get to the target. Represent strategies on a double number line. Students are challenged to determine the missing factor, when supplied with one factor and the product.

$$12 \times \square = 60$$
$$6 \times \square = 60$$
$$5 \times \square = 60$$
$$12 \times \square = 600$$
$$24 \times \square = 600$$
$$25 \times \square = 600$$
$$75 \times \square = 600$$
$$50 \times \square = 600$$

Behind the Numbers: How the String was Crafted

The first three problems are related, thereby supporting students to consider the relationship between multiplication and division. The first and third and the fifth and sixth problems use the commutative property. Doubling and halving relationships also are used.

Double Number Line · B9

Relating Multiplication and Division, Equivalence, Proportional Reasoning

This string uses a quotative model of division to examine the relationship between multiplication and division. Represent strategies on a double number line. Students are challenged to determine the missing divisor, when supplied with the dividend and the quotient.

$$60 \div \square = 5$$
$$60 \div \square = 6$$
$$60 \div \square = 12$$
$$600 \div \square = 12$$
$$600 \div \square = 24$$
$$600 \div \square = 25$$
$$600 \div \square = 50$$
$$600 \div \square = 75$$

Behind the Numbers: How the String was Crafted

The divisor 10 in the second problem must be halved to produce a quotient of 12 in the third problem. The fourth problem has a dividend that is 10 times as large as the dividend in the previous problem, so the divisor must be 10 times as large to maintain the equivalence of a quotient of 12. This type of proportional reasoning is required throughout the string.

Double Number Line · B10

Equivalence, Variation

This string of related problems is designed to encourage students to continue to use the open number line to represent algebraic problems and at the same time develop proper use of variables. Students should draw representations on paper as they go through the string. This is different than the usual practice of a teacher representing their strategies. Here they are being asked to draw in order to use the number line as a tool to think with.

Here is an unknown amount on a number line. I call it j.

Where is two times j?

Where is two times these two js?

Where is $4j - 6$?

Suppose I tell you that $4j - 6$ is the same as $2j$. What now?

How about $2j - 3$: Where is it? Why?

What if I told you that $4j - 6$ is the same as $3j$? What now?

Now where is $2j - 3$? Why?

Behind the Numbers: How the String was Crafted

The string is crafted to encourage students to represent algebraic expressions in relation to other related algebraic expressions, and to treat variables with variation. In the first problem, j is represented and $2j$ would be twice j. The next problem will probably also be easy for students. Now there are four equal jumps. When the third problem introduces −6, students may begin to comment that they don't know how big the jump is in relation to the steps. That is true, and such comments should be encouraged. Nevertheless, ask students to draw what they think at this time and to share a variety of representations. Their diverse representations will emphasize that this quantity is unknown, since the size of the jump could vary. The next problem introduces an equivalent expression that may be a surprise, and could cause students to have to redraw. As the string continues, new equivalents are introduced, causing further adjustments.

A Portion of the Minilesson

Inside One Classroom

Carlos (the teacher): *(Having drawn the number line without indicating any lengths—just one jump with a j above it—and then added the second jump.)* Rosie, show us where 2 times these 2 *j*s would be. *(Rosie draws two more jumps. Now there are four.)* Does everyone agree? *(Several comments of agreement.)* OK. So here's the next one. Where would 4*j* minus 6 be?

Heidi: You take 4—I mean 6 little steps back.

Juan: But how little?

Carlos: Good question. How little?

Heidi: I don't know exactly. They are just smaller than jumps, I think. *(Puts little steps on the diagram.)*

Juan: But maybe the jump is smaller even than 6 steps.

Sam: Or maybe the jump is really big, like 100!

Carlos: You're right. We don't know what *j* is, do we? Well, suppose I tell you that 4*j* minus 6 is the same as 2*j*.

Thomas: You tricked Heidi!

Carlos: I don't think so. Heidi didn't know the new information, so her diagram is correct for what we had then. What do we do now? Talk to your neighbor a bit about this.

Heidi: If 4*j* minus 6 is equal to 2*j*, then that means 2 jumps are equal to 6!

Juan: Here's how Tony and I fit them together. I think we have *j* equals 3 now!

Author's Notes

Now the two original jumps are followed by two more equivalent jumps.

By repeating Juan's question "How little?" Carlos gets the class to reflect on the relationship between the size of the unknown quantity and the length of one. (In fact, there is no relationship yet, and that will come up next).

Heidi has trouble answering an ambiguous question. The relationship is not known. But the representation can still capture the essence of 4*j* – 6 and her diagram does it.

With the additional information, the representation Heidi drew has to be modified, reflecting the nature of a variable and this type of representation. The class has seen this before, and the pair talk here allows them to revisit this big idea.

Juan and Tony have found the link and they are able to use the representation to see that the information forces *j* = 3.

Double Number Line · B11

Equivalence, Variation

This mental math minilesson has been crafted to support students in thinking about algebraic expressions in relation to other expressions. Each of the variables *x*, *y*, *a* and *b* is introduced on the number line. Then, in the rest of the string, students represent the answers by using or modifying that original drawing. In this minilesson variation is emphasized.

If this is x and if this is y, where would $3x + y$ be?

How about $2x + 2y$?

What if I told you $3x + y = 2x + 2y$.
What do you have to do with your representation?

Suppose this is a and I told you that $2a = 3b$. Show this.

Would $4a = 9b$ work? How would you represent it?

What about $16a = 27b$? Could you draw it on the same diagram?

OK, let's look at the original diagram, $2a = 3b$. What if $9b = 36$.

Can you find a?

Behind the Numbers: How the String was Crafted

The first problem introduces a representation for x and y. Draw x as a jump and y as a different size jump. Initially the sizes don't matter since they are variables and at this point their values are unknown. As you progress through the string, you will be forcing their values. The third question pushes students to redraw and to eliminate the equivalent pieces. For example, if students line up the jumps on the number line, two jumps of x can be eliminated, leaving $x + y = 2y$. So $x = y$.

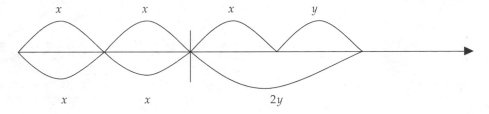

The next four problems are also related in order to cause students to think about the relationships. If $2a = 3b$, the next two problems are not possible. A big idea is at play here. Whatever you multiply one side of an equation by, you must also multiply the other side by, in order to maintain equality.

77 ÷ 7

707 ÷ 7

7007 ÷ 7

1212 ÷ 12

12012 ÷ 12

1212 ÷ 101

123123 ÷ 123

345345 ÷ 1001

2 × 3 × 5

4 × 7 × 5

2 × 6 × 25

2 × 9 × 15

2 × 7 × 6 × 5

4 × 11 × 25

4 × 9 × 75

11 × 3

101 × 3

1001 × 3

101 × 12

101 × 25

1001 × 123

1001 × 456

66 ÷ 3

606 ÷ 3

6006 ÷ 3

1212 ÷ 3

1212 ÷ 6

2412 ÷ 6

3666 ÷ 6

Extras Just for Fun

String · C1

Associative and Commutative Properties

This string consists of problems that have more than two factors and encourages students to examine the numbers and decide on a helpful grouping. Both the associative and commutative properties may prove helpful. Once groups are made, strategies such as halving and doubling may also be helpful.

$$2 \times 3 \times 5$$
$$4 \times 7 \times 5$$
$$2 \times 6 \times 25$$
$$2 \times 9 \times 15$$
$$2 \times 7 \times 6 \times 5$$
$$4 \times 11 \times 25$$
$$4 \times 9 \times 75$$

Behind the Numbers: How the String was Crafted

The numbers in the string have been chosen to allow for several different groupings. If the 2 and 3 are multiplied first, the first problem can be seen as 6×5 and then halved and doubled to 3×10. The problem can also be seen as $(2 \times 5) \times 3$ at the start. The last problem, $4 \times 9 \times 75$, may look difficult, but it is easier when seen as $(4 \times 75) \times 9 = 300 \times 9$. Or 36×75 can be halved and doubled to produce $18 \times 150 = 9 \times 300$.

String · C2

Distributive Property, Place Value, Partial Quotients

This string provides some interesting patterns to explore, a result of place value and the distributive property. After examining why they are happening, students can write their own strings that produce further interesting patterns.

$$11 \times 3$$
$$101 \times 3$$
$$1001 \times 3$$
$$101 \times 12$$
$$101 \times 25$$
$$1001 \times 123$$
$$1001 \times 456$$

Behind the Numbers: How the String was Crafted

Place value and the distributive property for multiplication over addition underlie these interesting patterns.

String · C3

Distributive Property, Place Value, Partial Quotients

This string provides some interesting patterns to explore. After examining why they are happening, students can write their own strings that produce further interesting patterns.

$$77 \div 7$$

$$707 \div 7$$

$$47{,}007 \div 7$$

$$1212 \div 12$$

$$12{,}012 \div 12$$

$$1212 \div 101$$

$$123{,}123 \div 123$$

$$345{,}345 \div 1001$$

Behind the Numbers: How the String was Crafted

Place value and the distributive property for multiplication over addition underlie these interesting patterns. See C4 for additional support.

String · C4

Distributive Property, Place Value, Partial Quotients

See C3 for details (above).

$$66 \div 3$$

$$606 \div 3$$

$$6006 \div 3$$

$$1212 \div 3$$

$$1212 \div 6$$

$$2412 \div 6$$

$$3666 \div 6$$